D0579589

About the Authors

Carol Bobrowsky founded Roebling Stock Farm and raised working dogs and American Quarter Horses from 1966 to 1982. She later established Mulberry Farm kennel in Dutchess County, New York and began raising AKC-registered American Cocker Spaniels and Miniature Schnauzers in the early 1990s.

Jim Gladden joined Mulberry Farm in 1996, primarily as its webmaster. At that time, Carol had become interested in hybrid Poodle crosses, particularly Schnoodles and Cockapoos. She quickly realized that Jim's master's degree in biology uniquely qualified him to work with her in developing and refining the Schnoodle hybrid by using her already established Miniature Schnauzer lines. Through their diligent work, Carol and Jim are striving to set the standard for the Schnoodle as a breed.

About Our Cover Dog

Meet Katie von Bow Wow, a one-year-old Schnoodle owned by Catherine and Steve Conrad. Katie was bred by the authors, Carol Bobrowsky and Jim Gladden of Mulberry Farm kennel. Katie's owners describe her as full of life, friendly and a charmer. She likes to play hard, run, jump and scout around in the back yard, but when she's finished with her many activities, a favorite of which is playing ball outdoors, she'll fall asleep in your lap like a little angel. Katie's favorite treats are Cheerios®.

Schnoodle

By Carol Bobrowsky & Jim Gladden

Schnoodles possess oodles of charm and intelligence—a true designer-dog dream.

Kennel Club Books®, the country's only major publisher of exclusively dog books, proudly presents its *Designer Dog Series™* to celebrate the Schnoodle's coming-out party. Continuing in its bold effort to produce a unique line of dog books, Kennel Club Books® releases the first ever books on the specific designer dog cross-breeds. The company has also released many *Special Limited Editions* and *Special Rare-Breed Editions* on various unusual breeds.

Visit the publisher's website at www.kennelclubbooks.com to read more about the unique library of books available to dog lovers around the world.

Acknowledgments

Many thanks to the wonderful breeders and owners whose dogs are featured in this book: Carol Bobrowsky, Catherine and Steve Conrad, Annie Fitzpatrick, the Geivett family, James Gladden, Barbara Henry, the Janeczek family, Dr. Lynne Liptay, Terra and Gregg Loden, the Mae family, the Mallette family, the Miller family, Curtis and Debbie Moon, Cassandra, Austin and McKenzie Nasta, the Peyzer family, David Reis, Laura and Bruce Schwartz, Cheryl Smith and Diane Stoffer.

KENNEL CLUB BOOKS®

Designer Dog
SERIES™

SCHNOODLE
ISBN: 1-59378-672-7

Copyright © 2006 · Kennel Club Books, LLC
308 Main Street, Allenhurst, NJ 07711 USA
Printed in South Korea

Photography by Mary Bloom
with additional photos by Isabelle Français.

All rights reserved. No part of this book may be reproduced in any form, by photostat, scanner, microfilm, xerography or any other means, or incorporated into any information retrieval system, electronic or mechanical, without the written permission of the copyright owner.

10 9 8 7 6 5 4 3 2 1

Contents

The Schnoodle is a delightful mix of small-breed favorites...

Development of the
Schnoodle

The earliest occurrence of

the Schnoodle form was most likely a breed developed in England known as the Truffle Dog. General consensus of the literature is that white Toy Poodles (developed by breeding the larger German or French white corded Poodles with the Maltese) were crossed with a small terrier breed to create the Truffle Dog. The sagacious intellect and keen sense of smell common to both the Poodle and terrier breeds, combined with the determined digging skills inherent to most terriers, resulted in a breed that was essentially perfect for sniffing out and unearthing the very valuable "gourmet fungus."

Because truffles are found in the soil closely associated with only certain species of trees in the wild, truffle hunters had to go wherever such trees were located, often involving trespassing onto (and digging up) restricted property. The white Truffle Dog was especially useful for this task, since "hunting" had to be conducted at night under the cloak of darkness to avoid detection by land owners—and other truffle poachers!

A renaissance in popularity of the Poodle-terrier form came about on the other side of the Atlantic in America in the 1980s. At least one professional dog breeder purposely began crossing pure-bred Miniature Schnauzers with pure-bred Toy or Miniature Poodles to produce first-generation (F_1) Schnoodles

Miniature Schnauzer crossed with Poodle.

The Lagotto Romagnolo is a modern-day Truffle Dog developed from water dogs in Italy.

and later bred unrelated pairs of these hybrids to produce subsequent multi-genera-tional (F_2, etc.) breed lines. Although no documentation can be found in printed form regarding the origin and development of this crossbreed, we believe that the first selective breeding of Schnoodles occurred in Minnesota.

Regardless of where the professional breeding and record-keeping of Schnoodles first occurred in the United States, the original goal among the breeders appears to have been to develop an allergy-friendly, mid-sized, long-lived and intelligent dog that was not prone to the health disorders found in many of the pure-bred lines of the Miniature Schnauzer and Poodle. By the late 1990s, Schnoodle popularity had grown noticeably as the Schnoodle was considered to be one of the up-and-coming new "designer" Poodle-mix breeds.

Intelligent, alert and
adorable—just a few of
the traits that endear
the Schnoodle to many.

Combining the best of two much-loved breeds...

Meet the

Schnoodle

Parent Breeds

T he first Schnoodles

documented in the United States were derived from breeding Miniature Schnauzers with Toy or Miniature Poodles. The mere use of adjectives like "miniature" and "toy" in describing parent breeds and/or lines of dogs, however, suggests that a thorough background description of each breed (and their variations) is in order to truly understand the Schnoodle.

Two outstanding breeds result in a handsome hybrid with so much to offer.

into one irresistible Schnoodle package.

SCHNAUZERS

There are three unique breeds of schnauzer: Miniature, Standard and Giant. All three breeds were painstakingly developed from multi-generational lines in the neighboring kingdoms of Württemberg and Bavaria in Germany. The outstanding physical conformation and keenness of the original breed (Standard Schnauzer) was maintained throughout the evolution of the schnauzer breeds that followed.

The Standard Schnauzer, which is the medium-sized breed, dates back as far as the 15th century. As its name implies, this is undoubtedly the oldest, and the prototype, of the three breeds. It is believed that the Standard Schnauzer is the product of crossings of the German *Pudel,* the old Wirehaired Pinscher and the German Wolfspitz. Although classified as terriers in the American dog-show ring from 1899 to 1945 because of their coat and stance, Standard Schnauzers were transferred

to the Working Group after authorities contended that the breed had served as cattle tenders, guard and yard dogs and (occasionally) ratters since the breed's inception.

Standard Schnauzers range in height from 18 to 20 inches at the withers (17 to 19 inches for females), are square in the proportion of body length to body height and are ruggedly built with respect to both muscle and skeletal frame. Their coat is double, consisting of a harsh, hard and wiry outer coat with a soft undercoat. The breed's coat colors are pepper-and-salt (or similar equal mixtures) and black. The breed's nature is a wonderful combination of unusual intelligence, reliability and high-spiritedness.

The Miniature Schnauzer, or "Mini," originated from the crossing of Affenpinschers with small-sized Standard Schnauzers some time in the mid- to late 19th century. The Mini was recognized as a separate breed in 1899 when it initially appeared in its own

The smallest of the schnauzers, the Miniature, is huge in personality and popularity.

show classes in Germany, its native land. Minis first came to the United States in 1925 and have grown steadily in popularity. It's noteworthy that the American Kennel Club (AKC) appears steadfast in classifying Minis as terriers (unlike their ancestor breed, the Standard Schnauzer), yet several authorities claim that there is no reason for this classification. Regardless, the Miniature Schnauzer has endeared himself to many owners as a delightful, attractive companion, as well as an excellent watchdog.

Minis range in height from 12 to 14 inches at the withers

The Mini's "Giant" cousin...

and the schnauzer original,
the Standard.

(the ideal size being 13.5 inches) and resemble their larger cousin, the Standard Schnauzer. Like the Standard, the Mini is large-boned, of sturdy build and nearly square in proportion of body height to length. Miniature Schnauzers also have a double coat consisting of a hard, wiry outer coat and a close undercoat. Coat colors of the Mini are pepper-and-salt, black-and-silver and solid black.

The Giant Schnauzer, or *Reisenschnauzer*, is the largest and most recently developed of the three breeds of schnauzer. Before further unearthing this breed's history, it should be noted that virtually all breeds of dog (including the schnauzers) were developed over time in close relation to the occupations of the dogs' owners. New breeds were carefully fashioned and nurtured with the primary goal of assisting their owners in their day-to-day lives. Geographic region, climate and living conditions of the

Allure of Designer Dogs

Poodle mixes, like the Schnoodle, Cockapoo, Labradoodle, Goldendoodle and more, have recently come into the spotlight and are quickly gaining in popularity. Each puppy is unique and offers the benefits of the Poodle heritage: intelligence, an easy-care coat and a nice temperament. The more and more people seek out these mixes, the more the breeders will produce them. One must watch out for poorly bred pups, though, as unscrupulous breeders will eagerly mix their breeding stock to fulfill pet-distributor orders. The designer-dog purchaser needs to be just as careful when purchasing his Poodle cross as he would be if purchasing a pure-bred.

A desirable designer hybrid, cuddling its way into the hearts and homes of dog lovers across America.

owners were also significant factors in breed development.

With regards to the origin of Giant Schnauzers, it has been documented that Bavarian cattlemen journeying to Stuttgart, Württemberg, became interested in the Standard Schnauzer and brought some of these powerful, medium-sized dogs back with them to Bavaria. Because the raising and selling of cattle, sheep and other livestock were major occupations in these regions of Germany, it was necessary for these dogs to assist the shepherds in driving their livestock to the marketplace. Bavarians collectively liked the Standard Schnauzer, as the sheepmen and other small-

livestock farmers found that this size of herding animal was quite ample for their needs. Cattlemen, however, discovered that they needed a larger breed for driving their cattle over the countryside to market.

It is believed that their first attempts at modifying this mid-sized terrier line to create a drover's dog involved crossing Standard Schnauzers with some of the smooth-coated dog breeds used by herdsmen and dairymen, as well as the Bouvier des Flandres. Rough-haired sheep dogs and finally the black Great Dane were then bred into this evolving terrier line to produce the powerful, highly intelligent, wiry-coated drover's terrier known as the Giant Schnauzer.

A rare litter indeed—giant Schnoodle pups whelped from a beautiful Giant Schnauzer and a Standard Poodle sire.

The *Münchener*, as the breed was called for many years, was renowned throughout southern Germany from the late 19th into the very early 20th century as an excellent cattle and droving dog. However, with the advent and expansion of mechanized transportation throughout Europe, cattle droving became a thing of the past. Although the breed was still used by butchers, at breweries and in stockyards in the different role of guard dog, it wasn't until just prior to World War I that the Giant Schnauzer drew nationwide attention in Germany as an excellent police dog.

The Giant Schnauzer was introduced into the United States in the 1920s, after World War I, and admitted into the AKC's Stud Book in 1930. Male Giant Schnauzers range in height from 25.5 to 27.5 inches at the withers; females range from 23.5 to 25.5 inches. The corresponding mid-range heights are desired. Like their two kin breeds, Giant Schnauzers are double-coated, with a harsh, dense, wiry outer coat and a soft undercoat. Their bodies are also nearly square in the proportion of body height at the withers to body length. Coat colors are solid black or pepper-and-salt. Their temperament is a combination of high-spiritedness and alertness with intelligence and extreme reliability.

POODLES

The Poodle, although classified in more recent times in the AKC's Non-Sporting and Toy Groups, has a long great history of being called upon by hunters to retrieve fallen game, most notably from the water. It has been suggested in literature by several breed historians that the genesis of the Poodle breed occurred as far back as the first century A.D. The "archaeo-Poodle" is thought to have been developed from crossing the white Maltese with the Spanish dog known as the spaniel. This is supported in part by the spaniel's affinity for water and the breed's renowned retrieving traits. Further, the documented friendly behavior of both of the Poodle's parent breeds is very likely a major contributing factor in the Poodle's temperament. This splendid combination could certainly account for the widespread popularity of the Poodle.

From around the 12th to the 15th century, Poodle-like dogs appeared in various forms of art and on coins from both Roman and Greek cultures. Three nations, Germany, Russia and France, later emerged as the "original" homes of this breed, each with slightly different variations of the Poodle. The German variety of the Poodle was more robust and heavy-boned and was bred for retrieving fallen game (e.g., ducks) from the water; hence, the name *Pudel*, which translates as "to splash in water." The Russian Poodle had a slighter, more refined build and served more as a companion dog. Poodles in France had an even loftier role in society, as many elite owners had their dogs' woolly, curly coats elaborately sculpted by fashion artisans.

Popularity of the breed spread to other countries in Europe but most notably "across the channel" to England. Historians have noted that breeds such as the English Water Dog, among others, were developed by crossing the Poodle with

A Toy Poodle trimmed to the nines in a dazzling coat of white...

and a more casual Miniature Poodle on the other end of the color spectrum.

established breeds in England. It was from England that the Poodle made its way across the Atlantic to the United States in 1887. By 1960, the Poodle achieved the number-one rank in AKC registrations and held that position for 23 consecutive years.

Much of the nearly worldwide admiration of the Poodle in more modern times can be attributed to the many variations in the breed's size and coat types, styles and colors. Similar to the schnauzer breeds, there are three sizes of Poodle: Standard, Miniature and Toy. With Poodles, however, the different sizes are all one breed of dog. The prototype of the Poodle breed is the Standard (largest). Poodles greater than 15 inches at the withers in height are deemed Standard Poodles. Those that are 15 inches or less in height but in excess of 10 inches at the withers are considered Miniature Poodles. Toy Poodles are 10 inches or under at the withers.

Coat types range from long, orderly cords to thick, dense curls, with the latter being most popular in modern times. Popular coat styles (primarily with the curly hair type) run the gamut, ranging from a short, nearly uniform length over much of the body (essentially, the "sporting" clip) to very elaborate, highly sculpted creations. The AKC specifies acceptable clips for showing, but sometimes pet owners use their imagination, with their dogs' hairstyles reflecting their own personal styles.

Coat colors accepted by the AKC for Poodles showing in competition nearly run the spectrum of possibilities, including black, blue, gray, silver, brown, café-au-lait, apricot and cream. According to the AKC standard, however, these colors must be even and solid throughout the coat. Outside the American show ring, many interesting color combinations such as "phantom" (black with tan markings or black with silver markings) and the various parti-colors (e.g., black and white, brown and white) add great variety to the full complement of today's breed.

Virtually all of the ancestors of today's Poodle were known to be good swimmers. However, one relative of the clan, known as the Truffle Dog, is no longer used in the water. Truffles, an edible fungus considered a very valuable delicacy to gourmets and non-gourmets alike, are found in the soil near specific tree species of the forest. Truffle hunting was fairly widely (though secretively) practiced in England and later in various countries on the European continent. Because of their small size and keen sense of smell, Toy Poodles were called upon to seek out and unearth these peculiar-yet-delectable morsels. Eventually, terriers (possibly schnauzers), known for their tenacious digging spirit, were crossed with these Toy Poodles to develop the Truffle Dog—and quite possibly the first Schnoodles.

Poodle plus Miniature Schnauzer equals trainability, playfulness, love of family and more.

Lounging around or hard at play...

Schnoodle

The Schnoodle—a cross between two beloved, centuries-old breeds—was created for different reasons than its parent breeds and is still in its infancy with respect to its development as a breed of its own. Both ancestral parent breeds were created for utilitarian purposes: the Poodle types were initially developed primarily to assist in hunting and sporting activities, and the schnauzer breeds were developed for herding cattle and later for guarding property. The desire for an allergy-friendly (i.e., low shedding, hypoallergenic), intelligent and mid-sized companion breed spurred breeders to conceive the Schnoodle hybrid. Results obtained thus far from the conscientious breeders involved in the Schnoodle's development are quite favorable, though with some expected variability.

A Schnoodle for all seasons!

the versatile Schnoodle appeals to many.

Variations can be found in the Schnoodle's size and coat type.

SIZE DIFFERENCES

There are three recognized sizes of Poodle: Standard, Miniature and Toy. A fourth size, the Teacup, is not recognized by the Poodle Club

SIZE

Schnoodles, like people, can grow up to be different sizes as adults, even those that come from the same litter. Some siblings can become quite larger than others, while others in the litter can remain "petite." This occasional disparity is basically a reflection of the size variability in the Poodle lines. As with Poodles and schnauzers, size classification of Schnoodles is based on body height at the withers and not on weight, due to the sometimes wide range of variation in otherwise "like" individuals. As with the Poodle, there are three types of Schnoodle based on size: standard (large), miniature (medium) and toy (small). Schnoodles taller than 15 inches at the withers are standard-type. Miniature-type Schnoodles are those that range from over 10 inches to 15 inches at the withers. Toy-type Schnoodles are 10 inches or less at the withers.

It never hurts to have big friends!

Part schnauzer, part
Poodle, part
mischief...

From the tip of his nose...

COAT TYPES AND COLORS

Like the parent breeds' coats, the Schnoodle's coat does not shed. Very little hair is lost from the coat on a day-to-day basis, and thus little dander is produced. This can be very helpful for allergy sufferers who would like to get a wonderful canine companion. The coat texture of today's Schnoodles can range from somewhat coarse (similar to the schnauzers) to soft (similar to the Poodle) or anything in between.

Schnoodle coat colors vary from some of the solid colors of the parent breeds (black or silver) to familiar combinations (black and tan or "phantom") to dilutions and/or blends of parent breed colors (faded apricot or faded sable with black tips). Similar to the parent breeds, coat colors can change drastically from puppyhood to adulthood. In such cases, not even the most experienced professional breeder can always and absolutely guarantee the color or shade that a puppy will become by the time he reaches one or two years of age.

TEMPERAMENT

The temperament of the Schnoodle generally reflects the best characteristics from the two parent breeds. Schnoodles are keenly intelligent and therefore are one of the easiest crossbreeds to train. Although this intelligence can cause them to be somewhat demanding of their owners' attention at times, Schnoodles are quite eager to learn and to please their owners/trainers. They are happy, affectionate, playful, clever and very amusing. Like their schnauzer ancestors, Schnoodles exhibit a very sensible, steady and human-like disposition. All of these qualities combine to rank them as excellent companions and family dogs.

This is not to imply, however, that Schnoodles have no challenging qualities to their temperaments. Schnoodles are often vocal and can produce sharp, piercing barks common to the schnauzer breeds. As with any other breed, if you respond properly to this type of barking and give your dog

to his docked furry tail, the Schnoodle is one-of-a-kind.

General Appearance

All three Schnoodle types are roughly square when considering the proportion of body length (measured from the withers to the base of the tail) to body height at the withers. They are of moderate to rugged build with respect to muscle and skeletal frame. As with schnauzers and Poodles, the Schnoodle's tail is docked at a very young age and the dewclaws are removed. The tail is set high on the posterior and is held happily erect when the Schnoodle is either at attention or walking. The muzzle is nearly square and of medium length, with a generous covering of facial hair. Teeth should form a scissors bite when the mouth is closed. The Schnoodle's ears are set fairly high on the head and are not cropped.

consistent positive training, your Schnoodle can quickly be taught when such barking behavior is not appropriate. Schnoodles are also like the schnauzers in that they are highly spirited and are very interested in being a part of the family—an "equal," so to speak.

One of the greatest hurdles to be overcome by today's dedicated, committed dog breeders is the all-too-common "opportunistic breeders" who market typically very poor-quality and sick "random crossbreeds" to the unsuspecting public. Given the relative ease, provided by the Internet, in marketing anything without any type of validation, opportunistic breeders are flooding the dog market with, at best, unhealthy mutts. For a breed of dog to be truly developed, a standard consisting of specific characteristics and requirements must be formulated and agreed upon by enough dedicated breeders to achieve consistency among and between generations.

This affectionate Schnoodle is
not afraid to show his feelings.

Schnoodle puppy love...

Finding a
Schnoodle
Breeder

The question "How do I find a good Schnoodle breeder?" should be a simple, straightforward one to answer. Unfortunately, very few things are simple anymore. First of all, there are proportionally few breeders who claim to breed Schnoodles. Secondly, of those people who *claim* to breed Schnoodles, only a very small percentage of them are dedicated, professional dog breeders who use high-quality parent breeding lines and who carefully nurture the puppies after they are born. A disturbingly large proportion of the dogs sold to consumers—pure-bred dogs and crossbreeds alike—are produced by less-than-ethical means.

There are plenty of irresponsible, uncaring people out there who breed dogs solely to produce as many puppies as possible, as cheaply as possible, and then sell them in quantity, often through a third party. These puppies come from inferior adult stock and sometimes are not even the breed or hybrid that is advertised by the "breeder." The puppies are usually raised in poor living conditions, frequently in outbuildings with very little or no human interaction. The puppies are not given adequate time to nurse on their mother, often being removed and sold at the tender age of just five weeks. These puppies have had a bad start in life, including poor nutrition and lack of rudimentary care (e.g., deworming, vaccinations, human handling). They are often

hanks to hard work, dedication and ethical breeding.

...and they call it Schnoodle love!

carriers of parasitic protozoa (e.g., *Giardia*, coccidian), worms, fleas, lice, mange and other mites. Although these things are all readily curable, puppies in poor condition can die from simple ailments that an otherwise healthy puppy could easily overcome.

Next, add to these factors that the parent dogs used to mass-produce puppies are not sound examples of their respective breeds and you have essentially all the makings of a potential disaster for unsuspecting buyers. No reputable professional dog breeder would breed dogs or raise puppies in this manner, without proper care and solely for profit.

Given that background information regarding disreputable breeders, how does a prospective Schnoodle owner find a reputable breeder? Since Schnoodles are not yet a standardized, recognized breed, finding a Schnoodle breeder can be more or less limited to researching the Internet and local newspapers and getting word-of-mouth referrals. At the present time, the best source is the Internet.

There are many websites dedicated to the Schnoodle, offering virtual classified-ad listings for available Schnoodles. Once these potential puppy sources are found, the prospective Schnoodle owner must figure out which of them are to be outright avoided and which ones may actually have wonderful, healthy Schnoodles to choose from. There are certain qualities that make potentially *good* breeders stand out from the rest. Here is a list of the most important things to look for, although not given in any particular order of importance:

Does the breeder allow visitors to see the kennel or area where the adult breeding dogs are housed and where the puppies are raised? If the answer to this is "no," move on to the next candidate on the list! Any breeder who states verbally or in an advertisement that "buyers or visitors cause puppies to become sick" or that seeing the kennel facilities, even from a distance, somehow compro-mises the welfare of the animals, is almost certainly hiding something.

Where are the puppies raised? Puppies raised in a kennel with little or no human contact are poorly socialized and can be timid, fear-aggressive and/or unaccustomed to ordinary household sounds and activities and therefore harder to train, housebreak and generally acclimate to the home environment. The ideal scenario is to find a breeder who has the dam deliver her puppies in the house and raises them in the home environment. Puppies reared in the home are usually handled, interacted with and kept clean, and they become used to common household noises such as the vacuum cleaner, telephone, television, radio, etc. These things are all part of the socialization process that helps to create a well-adjusted puppy. Such a scenario also means that the breeder cares about the welfare of the puppies.

Does the breeder own one or both parent dogs? If the

answer to this question is "yes," will the potential buyer be allowed to meet one or both of the parent dogs? It is possible and common that the sire is not owned by the breeder or is being leased out as a stud. In such a case, he might not be available for a personal inspection. It is also possible, in certain cases, for the dam (the bitch) to be leased or owned in a partnership and not be available once the puppies are weaned from her. Pictures of the mother dog nursing the puppies are not as good as the real thing but are certainly better than nothing at all (as is seeing pictures of the sire). If the parent dogs are AKC-registered or registered with some other recognized registry, copies of their papers should be made available for perusal. Customers can and should ask for copies of these papers.

Will the breeder give a potential customer a list of references? A good breeder should be able to and willing to give the prospective buyer a list of references. These would be people who have adopted or purchased puppies from that breeder over a period of a few years. The breeder should also make available the name of his veterinarian who has dealt with the breeder and knows the health history of the breeder's adult dogs as well as that of the puppies that the breeder has been raising and selling. If the breeder is not comfortable giving this information or flat-out refuses, it could mean that there are few, if any, happy customers or that the breeder has not provided proper veterinary care.

Is there a written guarantee? Although there are some states in the US that have puppy and dog "lemon laws" in place, most do *not*. While a written guarantee is only as good as the person/breeder who stands behind it, it's better to have a guarantee in writing than to not have one. If a puppy becomes sick, dies or shows signs of a genetic deformity within a specified period of time, the buyer would have no legal

Is the pups' area cozy and clean?

Does the breeder give the pups safe exposure to the world outside the whelping pen?

Every busy puppy needs time out to relax with Mom.

puppy must be returned to be euthanized. They do this knowing that most people will not want the puppy or dog they have grown to love put to sleep so, the "guarantee" essentially becomes meaningless (and the seller doesn't have to return any money).

Are the parent dogs healthy? It would be easy for any breeder to answer "yes" to this obvious question, but if the breeding dogs are available for viewing, the customer will know for sure whether they are healthy, friendly, clean and well-kept. Conversely, if the breeder has shallow excuses for keeping prospective buyers from seeing the adult dogs, the kennel and/or the rest of the litter of puppies, this should raise a bright red flag! The breeder should not just say that the parents are healthy, he should have their health records and health-testing documentation to prove it. Do not be shy about asking to see such

recourse without something in writing from the breeder. A good breeder will usually guarantee a puppy against any hereditary defects for at least one year, and this guarantee should be for a full refund of the purchase price or another puppy. The breeder should not ask for the defective puppy to be returned if a qualified, licensed veterinarian states in writing that the puppy will not be fit as a pet. Many times, unscrupulous breeders will stipulate that the original

The perfect pairing—youth and beauty.

paperwork, as a reputable breeder will have no problems showing it to you.

Are the puppies housed in clean surroundings? People who live in filth and expect their dogs and puppies to live in filth are usually lax in all things. Cleanliness goes hand in hand with good health. Fleas, ringworm, lice, mange mites and intestinal parasites thrive in a dirty environment. Breeders who require many days' notice before clients can visit, who will not let people see all of the puppies or who only take pictures of the newborn puppies are usually covering up bad conditions. If the puppies are taken care of properly, they should be available for assessment with very little advance notice.

Although it is impossible to have a kennel or puppy pen kept *perfectly* clean at all times, there are degrees to everything. If a place is so filthy that the customer is uncomfortable or is sickened by the sight (and smell) of the conditions, *that* is not the place to get a puppy.

Puppy Ownership

Anyone interested in taking on the responsibility of owning a puppy deserves a beautiful, healthy, well-socialized puppy. This should be the rule, not the exception!

When every Schnoodle face seems to say "Pick me!"...

Selecting a
Schnoodle
Puppy

Once you have finished your research and chosen a Schnoodle breeder, the next step is selecting a puppy. There will hopefully be more than one puppy to choose from in the litter, but this is not always the case. Sometimes litters of puppies can be quite small, or perhaps most of the puppies in a litter have already been spoken for by the time you contact the breeder. In other cases, the breeder takes the time to gather specific information about inquiring customers and their families to help take the guesswork out of picking a puppy. Since the breeder typically has a good idea about each puppy's general behavioral and size characteristics by the time prospective buyers are allowed to visit and handle the pups, the information gathered from each customer can guide the breeder in determining which puppy or puppies may be the best fit for each client.

Although many prospective buyers would love to select their puppy by visiting the breeder, playing with all of the puppies and choosing between several candidates, this is *not* the best way of choosing a puppy from the *puppy's* perspective. Young puppies do not have a lot of stamina. If many families, including children, come to play with and pick out puppies on a given day, the puppies will be over-stimulated and over-tired and can become susceptible to illnesses. Even if customers arrive on

you need to make a well-thought-out decision.

RECOGNIZING A KNOWLEDGEABLE BREEDER

A knowledgeable breeder will maintain a clean, healthy environment for all dogs and puppies. The puppies will be socialized from an early age, receiving the attention and handling they need from the breeder. The puppies will also have received appropriate worming treatments and vaccinations prior to being allowed to leave the breeder's premises. A responsible breeder will also make sure that his puppies go to good homes. Be ready to be scrutinized prior to being allowed to purchase a pup.

schedule for their appointed visit with a litter of puppies, puppy behavior can be very misleading. The friskiest puppy or puppies, at that given time, may have just woken up from a nap, while the calmest of the litter may simply be exhausted from extensive playing. For these reasons, it is crucial that the buyer ask the breeder for input about the individual puppies during the selection process.

Given that all of the litter-mates are well rested when you visit a breeder to choose a puppy, watching the puppies interact with one another is a good way to gauge which puppy or puppies are more "alpha" (dominant) and which are more laid-back. Puppies who have nursed together and grown up together have typically established their own social hierarchy or pecking order. If observed carefully, it is usually possible to see which puppies are more aggressive with their litter-mates and which are the mellow ones. There *are*, however, instances in which siblings are all nearly even-tempered and no alpha puppy can be easily identified. Although many people go looking for a puppy with a specific set of characteristics already in mind, such as male versus female, a particular coat color or pattern of markings, the largest pup in the litter or the runt, etc., a puppy's personality and disposition should be the ultimate deciding factors when making your choice from a healthy litter.

We should mention here that "runt" does not mean that the puppy will remain the smallest. This term is a misnomer. It does not mean that the puppy will be the smallest, the cutest or anything else associated with the term. All puppies grow to their genetically "pre-programmed" size. Some puppies in a litter simply had the least amount of space in the womb to grow or received less nourishment during fetal development or while nursing after birth. In actuality, given proper food and care, the runt

of a litter can grow to become the *largest* in the litter.

Once you have observed the puppies interact with each other, it is time to choose one or two pups to play with and hold. This is a good time to see how a particular puppy reacts to being taken away from his littermates. You will want to see that a puppy is frisky, outgoing and playful when on

the floor, yet calm and affectionate while being held. Curiosity and lack of fear are indicative that a puppy has been well socialized and has not been traumatized during his short life. When a clapping sound or other unusual noise is made, a puppy should come toward the person making the sound. Not only does this show that a puppy is inquisitive and friendly but it also tells the buyer that the puppy can hear and see.

Puppies should have clean, shiny coats. Their eyes should be bright and clear (not bloodshot or pink), with no mucus-like discharge. There should also be no evidence of discharge from the puppy's nose. Remember, dogs do *not* get colds in the way that humans think of colds. If a puppy has nasal discharge, runny eyes and/or any signs of diarrhea or an elevated temperature (unusually warm nose), you should not consider buying any puppy from that particular breeding establishment. These are symptoms of serious illnesses such as distemper or parvovirus, which are contagious among dogs and can quickly kill a puppy.

Who will be top pup in the pack? Observe the littermates in action and watch personalities emerge.

Puppies who are lethargic, who do not attempt to play, who are not interested in their surroundings and who are not interested in investigating new people and new toys are puppies who have health problems or serious social problems. Puppies who cower, run for cover and hide, crawl on their tummies or continuously tremble when held, no matter how long they are held, are puppies who have not been properly socialized and may be hard to train. Fearful puppies are some of the most difficult to work with, because many times they are so withdrawn that any attempt to teach them even the simplest things can be misconstrued by the puppy as punishment.

Literature abounds with various methods for temperament-testing young puppies. Prospective puppy buyers often read one or more of the best-selling books about the proper ways to choose a puppy, etc. They then go to the breeder and expect that they will be allowed to follow the instructions from these books and turn one or more puppies upside down or on their sides to check behavioral responses and to perform various other tests. Whereas these tests *may* show tendencies in a puppy's personality or demeanor, the responses of the puppy to a particular battery of tests may be misinterpreted or taken out of context by the prospective buyer and not be meaningful whatsoever. If, for example, a young puppy has never been subjected to certain actions, and these actions are conducted in a manner that frightens the puppy, there can be false conclusions made about that puppy. Perfectly acceptable puppies can (and have been) branded as "incorrigible" or "unfit as pets." It is up to the customer to ask the breeder if he temperament-tests his puppies and, if so, what degree of testing has been done.

If a breeder uses gentle dogs in the breeding

program, and the puppies have been raised in a social environment, most puppies will grow up to be fine dogs. Certain puppies that are more active than others *may* require a bit more patience, time and training but should grow up to be good dogs. Again, by carefully watching the puppies play and interact with each other, much can be learned about their general behavior. Based on the size and type of family that the puppy will be joining, and the lifestyle of this family, the breeder should be able (and willing) to offer sound advice to the prospective buyers.

Because the Schnoodle is a crossbreed, there are no exact standards for appearance to go by when selecting a puppy. The customer cannot determine by looking at the parent dogs what the puppies may look like when they are fully grown. This is a good time, however, to check the parent dogs and make sure that they are sound and healthy. In this particular case, are the

Miniature Schnauzer and Poodle parents each a seemingly good representative of their breed? If you are not knowledgeable as to what these dogs should look like, you should do some research and familiarize yourself with pictures and descriptions of the parent breeds. We have also offered such descriptions in this book. If both parents look like the good breed representatives that you've seen in pictures and are healthy, friendly and gentle, you will have a much better likelihood of getting a good Schnoodle puppy who will grow up to be a good pet for you and your family.

You might also want to ask the breeder for pictures of any Schnoodles previously raised and sold. Good breeders keep in touch with their puppy owners whenever possible and usually have pictures of pups sold in the past, as well as follow-up pictures of the pups as grown dogs. Many times, the puppies being looked at are from a repeat breeding, meaning from a sire and dam that have been mated together previously. Seeing pictures of grown siblings from previous litters can give you a very good indication of what your new puppy will look like when fully matured. All puppies are thought to be cute, but it is very wise to consider what the adult dog will be like with respect to size, color, general appearance and intelligence. This is especially true with crossbreeds.

Many breeders and laypeople alike say that crossing two breeds *cannot* give a true, reliable look to the offspring. After many years of crossbreeding certain types of dogs, we have come to the conclusion that if *high-quality, good representatives* of the parent breeds being crossed are used, the first-generation puppies in the litters produced tend to look *very much alike*, and subsequent litters from the same parents also take on identical or very similar characteristics. It is good to

remain open-minded insofar as coat color is concerned, because many of these Poodle crosses can, and do, change color dramatically from the time they are puppies to the time that their mature coats come in. Size too can sometimes only be guesstimated due to the fact that Poodles (especially the Toy and Miniature varieties) have been crossed for years, resulting in Miniature Poodles' being capable of producing Toy *and* Mini offspring and Toy Poodles' potentially producing pups who can grow much larger than their parents.

Pucker up, Mom!

How exciting for a family...

Basic Care of Your
Schnoodle

Assuring that your puppy or adult dog receives the proper diet throughout each stage of his life is one of the most important aspects of Schnoodle healthcare. Similar to the human body, if a dog's body doesn't receive sufficient amounts of vital nutrients for an extended period of time, his immune system could become weakened, thus threatening many aspects of his health and longevity. However, with scores of dog-food advertisers working the media today, trumpeting their enormous arrays of brands and varieties, it has become perplexing to choose which one is the best or right food for your dog.

An adorable pair, and best friends too!

to share their home and lives with a Schnoodle!

NUTRITION AND FEEDING
Let's begin with the types of dog food that are generally available on the market. The three mainstream types of dog food marketed to the general public are canned, semi-moist and dry. A fourth type of dog-food diet, which has somewhat recently become available in the refrigerator/freezer section in some pet-food specialty stores, is called the BARF (Biologically Appropriate Raw Food) diet, which was first developed by Australian veterinarian Dr. Ian Billinghurst. A form of the diet most typically seen in the United States is based on feeding a thoroughly ground mixture of raw meaty bones, raw vegetables, raw offal (entrails and internal organs of

Order me a giant bucket. Here's a growing litter of giant Schnoodles.

What dog doesn't
love dinnertime?

Thrown into the Schnoodle
mix is a little bit of hound...
"chow-hound," that is.

butchered animals) and supplements. This food typically comes in the form of patties, which can be either broken up into bite-sized pieces for the dog or served whole.

Essentially, proponents of the BARF diet cite that dogs did *not* evolve eating foods largely composed of grain-based filler carbohydrates with various quantities of cooked animal products and by-products, along with preservatives and artificial colors and flavors. Some veterinarians and other researchers have discovered evidence that some dogs exhibiting skin problems and other disorders were actually allergic to the grain and/or other ingredients and preservatives in the main-stream commercial dog foods and that the BARF diet was a good alternative.

There are, however, some less-than-favorable aspects to this raw-food diet as well. If purchased (or homemade) fresh or frozen, once it has thawed, it has a short refriger-ator-life before it starts to spoil. BARF food is also notably more expensive than the preserved commercial products. Perhaps a more concerning danger with such raw meat products is the threat of bacterial contamina-tion (e.g., Salmonella and *E. coli* strains), which can also be passed along and pose a life-threatening risk to young children, the elderly and people with compromised immune systems.

Getting back to the three mainstream commercial types of food—canned, semi-moist and dry—most puppies and adult dogs do not show any signs of allergies or other conflicts with *good* commercial dog foods. Pressure from BARF-diet researchers and other proponents has influenced some dog-food manufacturers to reconsider the ingredients/proportions that they put into their brand-name foods, as well as to come out with new alternative lines of food for more conscientious dog owners.

The quality of a commer-cial dog food can be judged by

the list of ingredients on the side of the package: if the first two or three ingredients are "whole meats" (e.g., chicken, turkey, lamb or beef), followed by meat by-products, grains and/or vegetables and other supplements, the product is very likely a *good* dog food. As a rule, the first few ingredients listed constitute the largest proportion of the food. An example of an ingredients list from a *good* (dry) dog food is: "Chicken, turkey, chicken meal, turkey meal, wholegrain brown rice, etc." If, however, the list of ingredients begins with "Lamb meal, ground millet, ground brown rice, canola oil...," or, worse yet, "Cornmeal, chicken by-product meal, soybean meal, animal fat...," keep looking and do not settle for anything less than a good-quality food.

The ingredients-list rule generally applies to all commercially produced dog foods. As for which of the three types of commercial food to choose, we have found that, after breeding and caring for dogs for nearly 40 years, the dry (kibble) food has been the best overall. The dry food isn't nearly as messy with respect to getting in the dog's facial hair while eating. It has also been suggested that the canned and semi-moist types of food may build tartar on the dog's teeth more readily. However, as long as the owner provides adequate dental care for his dog, there is little to no difference between a *good* canned food and a *good* dry food.

With regards to which formula of food to feed your Schnoodle, the vast majority of good dog-food manufacturers have age-specific foods available. Nutrient requirements (i.e., amounts of protein and fat that a dog needs in his food) of a dog change as a dog progresses from puppyhood to adulthood to his senior years. Puppies, for example, require a higher percentage of proteins and fats in their diet because their bodies are growing rapidly and puppies are simply much more active. It is definitely in the dog's best interest that you follow the

A DESIGNER DIET FOR ALL DOGS

Few dogs thrive on corn-based diets. You will rarely see a dog choose an ear of corn over a piece of meat. Dogs are carnivorous and therefore require the majority of their food to be meat-based. A quality dog food should contain meat as the main ingredient, and the remaining ingredients should include vegetables, brewer's yeast/rice, vitamins and omega fatty acids. Preservatives may be a sign that rancid ingredients were used in the manufacturing of the food and can also be damaging, over time, to your dog's internal organs.

Veterinarians and breeders will normally steer their clients to either the brand they sell or have been using with their own dogs. Ask them why that particular food is one they recommend. What are the key nutrients? Why will this particular food give the dog a glowing coat and spring in his step?

All dogs need love, care and...protein!

manufacturer's recommendations regarding the proper age-specific food "formula" for your dog.

The frequency of daily feedings (i.e., number of meals per day) for puppies is a rather highly debated issue among breeders and veterinarians. First of all, it is an age-dependent issue: puppies require more meals per day than adult dogs do because of the puppies' rapidly growing bodies. Many veterinarians profess that puppies should be fed at least three meals per day. Feeding puppies too many times a day, though, leads to most of them never finishing all of the food given to them at any meal. A more problematic issue that arises from feeding a puppy too many times a day is that it invariably causes the puppy to need to defecate more frequently, making the crate-training/housebreaking process that much more difficult—for both the puppy and the owner! Again, from decades of dog-breeding experience, we have concluded

that puppies only need to be fed twice daily, basically at the owner's breakfast time and dinner time.

One very important topic that must be mentioned deals with switching foods. Changing food brands and/or types in your dog's diet can upset his stomach considerably. This is especially true with puppies. Puppies generally are much more sensitive to food changes, so it is *strongly recommended* that a new puppy owner should not switch the puppy completely (i.e., all at once) from one food to another. If changing his food, make about a 50/50 mixture of the old food brand and the new food brand, and feed this to the puppy for several meals to gradually accustom his stomach to the new food. This is especially important when you first bring your puppy home from the breeder. If possible, keep the puppy on the same food that the breeder had been feeding him for at least the first several days after he comes home. Of course, there may be no reason to change his diet. If the breeder was feeding the puppy a good-quality food, then it is sensible to continue using that same food brand.

The actual amount of food given to the Schnoodle puppy at each meal will depend on the puppy's age and size. For example, an eight-week-old Schnoodle puppy can usually eat approximately one-third to one-half cup of dry food twice a day. As the puppy progressively gets a little older and larger, you will need to increase the amount of food per meal accordingly, perhaps in quarter-cup increments.

By the time the Schnoodle reaches the age of about seven months, he has essentially reached his adult height and length. You can at this point cut back the feeding frequency to once a day, preferably to just the morning feeding time. Try giving the young adult dog the same (total) daily amount of food that he was being given before. For instance, if the Schnoodle was eating three-quarters of a cup of dry food twice a day, switch to feeding him a cup-and-a-half once a day. Monitor the adult dog's body weight and build; if he maintains a good solid build, continue feeding that amount of food. If you can easily feel the dog's ribs under his skin, then the amount of food should be increased a little. If, on the other hand, it becomes difficult to feel his ribs, perhaps the amount of food should be reduced a bit.

As with people, each dog's metabolism is usually a little different; some require more calories to maintain the body's normal function, whereas others require notice-ably less. One very good way to prevent your Schnoodle from becoming overweight (and possibly incurring other health problems) is to avoid feeding him table scraps and other human food. In addition, some foods that people eat (e.g., pork, onions, chocolate, grapes, raisins, nuts and others) can actually be very harmful to dogs.

WATER

Adequate availability of water is as important to a dog as is access to food. Similar to the human body, a dog's body requires water for maintaining tissue hydration, digestion, metabolism, tissue growth and repair, etc. Dogs should have access to water at each meal (especially if dry food is used in his diet) and at least several other times during the day, depending in part on the age of the dog, the dog's activity level and the temperature of the dog's surroundings. It should be remembered that all town or city water coming into most homes has been chemically treated with chlorine compounds to neutralize bacteria, etc., in order to make the water safe for *human* consumption. However, these chlorine compounds can upset and irritate the gastrointestinal tract of puppies, causing bouts of diarrhea until their systems can adapt to the chemicals. This situation can lead to dehydration of the puppy and could even kill him. It is recommended that, if the new owner's home doesn't have a charcoal filtration system for the water (to remove chlorine and other elements), bottled spring water be purchased to give to the puppy. After a week or so of giving bottled water, the puppy can be slowly switched over to drinking tap water by offering a 50/50 mixture of bottled and tap water for a few days before changing completely to tap water.

When a puppy is being crate-trained or housebroken, access to water (other than at

Fresh water is a part of a dog's diet, too.

mealtimes) is somewhat limited by the training schedule to help the puppy gain better control of his bladder. When a puppy (or dog of any age) is involved in a lot of physical activity or exercise, more access to water is needed because of the moisture lost while panting. Since a dog's body cannot perspire to help cool himself (as a human's can), the animal's first recourse is to pant, which allows the body to exchange hot, moist air (as he exhales) for cooler air (as he inhales), thus reducing the core temperature of the body. This holds true also when room temperature is elevated or if the dog is outside in the sun for a period.

When providing water to a dog, the water should be clean and cool. The water bowl should be cleaned frequently as well (at least once a day). Owners should prevent their dogs from drinking water from puddles, pools or flowerpots. In the case of puddles in or near a lawn or field, herbicides and/or insecticides, which may have been applied to the grass, can

Excellent care pays off in a vibrant, handsome pet dog.

wash off and accumulate in such puddles. Many lawn fertilizers can even be a potential hazard. This is another reason why dog owners shouldn't allow their pets to mouth and/or eat grass or leaves. Even gnawing on a seemingly "harmless" stick can accidentally cause a chunk of the wood or heavy bark to become lodged in the dog's throat, stomach or intestines, typically requiring emergency surgery at a veterinarian's office or animal hospital.

EXERCISE

Like their Miniature Schnauzer and Poodle parent breeds, Schnoodles require a good structured exercise and interaction program with their owners. Regular daily walks on a leash are one good form of exercise, with the distance of the walks being dependent on the dog's age and size. Very importantly, Schnoodle puppies under the age of 16 weeks should not be taken for walks in public areas (e.g., on neighborhood sidewalks, in city parks, etc.) until after they have received the last of their puppy immunization shots, as they don't develop full immunity without the entire series of shots. Until the puppy is fully inoculated, he can get plenty of exercise during the interaction/play periods of his crate-training/housebreaking schedule, either exclusively indoors (for city-dwelling families) or with a combination of indoor activities and outdoor activities in the secured yard.

Once a puppy has all of his immunizations, his owners can begin to take him for relatively short walks (down the block to the corner and back again) on a leash. As the Schnoodle gets a bit older and continues to grow, the distance of his walks on a leash can be increased accordingly. Keep in mind, however, that puppies and young adults can be over-exercised and this could impair the proper develop-ment of certain bone joints/sockets, such as the hips. Schnoodles in puppyhood and young adulthood should not be allowed to run up and down staircases or frequently jump on and off furniture. Outside in the yard or park, though, playing catch with a ball or Frisbee® is a wonderful form of both physical and mental exercise. Exercise in the form of games that stimulate the Schnoodle's mind as well as his body are especially good, since a bored dog will typically find *something* to do to entertain himself—and that something is often something mischievous!

The Schnoodle loves to have a playmate...

and a safe yard in which to play, romp and explore.

Who says dogs and cats can't be friends?

SOCIALIZATION

Proper socialization of Schnoodle puppies with people, their littermates and other animals should begin early, preferably while they are still with the breeder. From the day that new puppy owners visit the breeder to the day they pick up their new Schnoodle, it's very important that they interact calmly and kindly with the pup yet remain in control of the puppy's actions (to gain the alpha position in the relationship).

Studies have indicated that puppies go through a series of behavior-development stages during the first 12 weeks of their lives and that these stages are extremely important in shaping a puppy's personality and his ability to interact with other creatures, including people. It is widely believed that puppies go through what is referred to as a fear/avoidance period between the ages of 8 and 10 weeks—a period that overlaps with the time when many breeders send their puppies home with new owners. When a family visits a breeder to choose a puppy from a litter, a puppy that acts very spirited and outgoing at seven weeks of age can, just a week later, act timidly and/or be afraid of the same visitors when they come to take the puppy home.

Bones and Boomer are a double dose of joy for their lucky family.

Although this may cause some prospective owners to have serious reservations about taking this particular puppy home, it is a natural part of the puppy's behavior and social development. It is important for new owners to behave toward the puppy as if nothing is out of the ordinary and to continue with tempered, positive interactions.

Puppies are very impressionable during their first few months of life. You should gradually introduce friends and family, including children, to your new Schnoodle, encouraging them to gently pet and interact with him. Perhaps after a few days, introduce one of your friends' or family members' dogs to your Schnoodle puppy. If possible, take your puppy along with you while you do your daily errands (for instance, in a lightweight soft-sided pet carrier), introducing him to the many people who will likely stop and ask you about your "new baby." This is an excellent way to expose your puppy to as broad a spectrum of human personalities, sizes, ages and ethnicities as possible. However, we reiterate that an important thing to keep in mind when you take a young puppy around with you is that he does not yet have full immunity to several potentially life-threatening diseases/viruses and will not have this immunity until he has received all of his puppy immunizations, typically at 16 weeks of age. Be certain that any dogs you allow your puppy to interact with are healthy, fully inoculated and up-to-date with their booster shots. Carry him when out and about rather than letting him walk on public sidewalks and grasses. Once your Schnoodle puppy has received all of his puppy immunizations and his first rabies shot (typically around the same age that he gets his last puppy shot), you can begin taking him to public parks and dog-walk areas to further expand his social awareness—and to have more fun!

Just like most children, your puppy will almost certainly test your authority (and patience) by deliberately repeating bad behaviors that you routinely correct him for (e.g., nipping at fingers). Although the puppy's incredible cuteness will constantly tempt you and your family

members to just give in and accept anything that the pup does, be it good or bad, *everyone* must remain strict with the training rules in order to properly teach your puppy. Each family member must give the same training commands to the puppy in the same way (and accept the same responses as correct) or the pup will become confused. This consistent behavior and set of standards also help to maintain the hierarchy in the family, with the *people* always remaining in the alpha position.

Another aspect of socialization is how well the puppy or dog deals with being by himself for more than just a few minutes (aside from bedtime). The amount of time and attention that you put into training and nurturing your Schnoodle must be balanced with reassuring him that being by himself is okay as well. Within a day or two after you first bring your puppy home from the breeder, you can start by leaving your puppy alone indoors in his training crate or exercise pen for a period of about ten minutes *after* you've taken him outside to go potty. Make sure that he has some sturdy safe toys to keep him occupied and then just give him a happy "goodbye" before you leave the room. You can either set up a small tape recorder outside the puppy's contained area before you leave the room to listen in on what he does when you leave or even set up a video camera to record his behavior. After ten minutes elapse, come back into the room as if nothing has happened, without paying any extra attention to the puppy. Check your tape and see how the puppy reacted. You can then try this same routine again, but this time you will leave your home completely instead of just leaving the room. Over the next few weeks, you can gradually increase the amount of time that you leave the puppy alone as long as it doesn't interfere with the puppy's crate-training or housebreaking schedule.

Abby is a smiling social butterfly.

GROOMING

The first step in grooming your Schnoodle is *frequently* combing his entire body with a good stiff-toothed (preferably steel) dog comb. This is *not* to be confused with brushing! Brushes are fine for quick touch-ups either after or between the times that you comb your dog or puppy. The best type of all-purpose brush for the typical Schnoodle coat is a pin brush. A slicker brush may also be used for puppy or shorter hair. However, only combs can reliably get all the way down through your Schnoodle's coat to the skin, where most tangles and mats in the hair start.

It is strongly recommended that owners begin regularly combing their new puppy soon after bringing him home from the breeder. This can be accomplished by combining social interaction with the combing activity. If you begin right away with getting the puppy accustomed to frequent combing, he will associate it with a pleasant experience and enjoy the routine. It also prevents knots from forming in the coat. All parts of the dog's body need to be

"Look ma, no tangles!"

Brushing promotes good looks and good health.

combed—the head, ears, neck, legs (including the armpits), paws, tail, chest, tummy, etc. To help prevent stressing your puppy or dog during combing, it is recommended that you alternate between the regions of the body that you work on. For example, start by combing the tail, then switch to combing the front right leg, the chest and so on. It is *very* important to always comb out the dog's hair *before* you give him a bath, since water (and subsequent drying) will make any tangles in the hair turn into mats, which are virtually impossible to fix other than by scissoring them out from the surrounding hair. Pre-bath combing also removes any dead hair from the coat, which would otherwise cause matting problems.

Bathing your puppy or adult dog usually doesn't need to be done more frequently than about once a month, depending on the day-to-day activities of your dog. Only use puppy shampoo for young dogs and regular dog shampoo for adult dogs. These shampoos are designed for dogs' very sensitive skin. Many pet shampoos have no detergent in them whatsoever, unlike typical shampoos designed for people. Even our "no-tears" baby shampoos are a bit too harsh for use on puppies and dogs. A kitchen or utility sink is usually adequate for bathing a puppy (or smaller dog), especially if the sink has a spray hose.

Before placing the pup in the sink, start the water running to get the temperature comfortably warm. You can help avoid getting water in the dog's ears by rolling two small cotton balls and inserting one into each of his ears, being very careful not to penetrate the ear canal. Place the puppy in the sink and gently wet his entire head first, then work your way back to his tail,

Sitting patiently for a salon visit with young groomers-in-training.

wetting the rest of his coat. Quickly drizzle the shampoo onto the puppy's coat from the neck to the tail; pour a little into one hand and then begin to lather the shampoo into the hair on his back, chest and abdomen. Pour a little more into your hand and carefully lather the puppy's head, including the ears and snout, avoiding getting any shampoo into his eyes or nostrils. Make sure that you lather shampoo down his entire legs and paws, including between the paw pads.

Thoroughly rinse the lathered soap from the entire coat, starting with the head and working your way down the neck to the back, chest, abdomen and tail. Lastly, continue down the legs to the feet. It's important to rinse *all* of the shampoo out of the coat. Next, gently massage and squeeze the excess water out of the hair, proceeding in the same order that you applied the shampoo. After removing the cotton from the puppy's ears, wrap him up in a warm, dry bath towel and gently pat

him with it to absorb as much of the water from the coat as possible. Continue drying with a second towel; having another dry towel is handy and speeds up the drying process. Get the pup as dry as possible with the towels. As long as the room temperature is adequately warm, the puppy can simply air-dry the rest of the way. A hand-held or fixed-stand hair dryer set on "low" or "medium" heat can be used to facilitate drying, but this most often causes the dog's hair to dry with less curl or wave in it. Whichever way that the hair is dried, it should be brushed out again following the bath.

Nail care of your Schnoodle puppy can begin soon after you bring him home from the breeder, even if the breeder had clipped the puppy's nails for you before you picked him up. While holding, petting and social-izing with your puppy, it is important to calmly take each of his paws into your hand, one by one, and massage the paw, even stroking each nail for a moment. This will help to make the puppy comfortable with you handling his feet to the point where he will trust you. Aside from gaining your dog's trust in letting you handle his sensitive feet, this is also an excellent way for you to check the length and condition of his nails. When a dog's nails get too long, they become much more prone to accidents such as getting caught in the carpet and tearing or scratching you or a family member while playing. Also, as the nails become long, the quick inside the base of the nail grows out farther and farther toward the tip. This makes it more difficult to adequately cut the nails without hurting the dog and causing the nail to bleed, possibly creating a traumatic experience for the puppy.

Nail clippers designed specifically for pets are available at most pet stores. For clipping the nails of a Schnoodle puppy, you can purchase a cat nail clipper, which is designed for dealing with smaller, thinner nails. A regular canine nail clipper is suggested for dealing with the thicker nails of an adult Schnoodle. It is also a good safety precaution to purchase styptic powder, which can be easily applied to a too-closely cropped nail to stop the bleeding (and also serve as an antiseptic) if the quick is accidentally nicked.

To clip the dog's nails, pick him up by the chest and sit down in a chair, holding the dog upright in your lap with his back toward you. Talk nicely to your dog, holding one of his paws in one hand and the nail clipper in the other. Gently push any hair at the tip of the paw backwards, away from the nails, to fully expose them. Holding your dog's leg as still as possible, quickly clip off the outer portion (tip) of each nail. It's better to be conservative with the amount of nail that you clip off rather than to clip too much and accidentally cut into the quick. You can always go back after you are done clipping and use a rough emery board or nail file to

Accustom your Schnoodle to regular pedicures.

shorten and smooth the nail tips. It's actually good practice to gently file the nail tips a little after clipping anyway, since cutting with nail clippers invariably leaves a sharp edge on the nail.

Cutting and trimming your puppy's or dog's hair is usually best left to a professional dog groomer who will (ideally) cut your dog's hair exactly per your instructions. If you have friends who are also dog owners, ask them for a referral to a good groomer if possible. Your dog's breeder may also groom or be able to refer you to a qualified groomer. If, however, you decide that you would like to learn how to groom your dog yourself, you will need to make an initial investment in a decent grooming table, an electric clipper with a few different-sized clipper blades, good grooming scissors and other grooming equipment. It is best in the long run to spend a bit more money and buy good-quality equipment at the outset. You can probably get the best

guidance regarding these purchases and proper care for the equipment from whoever is going to show you how to groom your dog. An occasionally discouraging aspect of home grooming is that it takes time and patience to learn the proper techniques. There will likely be some bad-hair days for your dog during your learning process. The positive side is that hair grows back!

Keeping your Schnoodle's ears clean and healthy is another important aspect of general canine care. Hair grows on the underside of the ear as well as on the top and even inside the ear canal itself. The hair growing on the underside of the ear nearest the ear canal should be groomed close to the skin to minimize the risk of moisture becoming trapped within the ear, which creates a favorable environment for fungal and mite infection. The hair growing from within the ear canal should be carefully plucked out by either an experienced groomer or your veterinarian, followed by the application of special drying powder to the ear canal. Dog owners can readily clean the undersides of the ears and around the openings of the ear canals using cotton balls dampened with ear-cleaning solution. This is available from your veterinarian and many pet-supply stores.

If the inner area of your dog's ear smells rather strongly and looks reddened, dirty or irritated, you should have your dog examined by your veterinarian as soon as possible. Other signs of ear problems are indicated by your Schnoodle's frequently scratching at his ears and/or shaking his head.

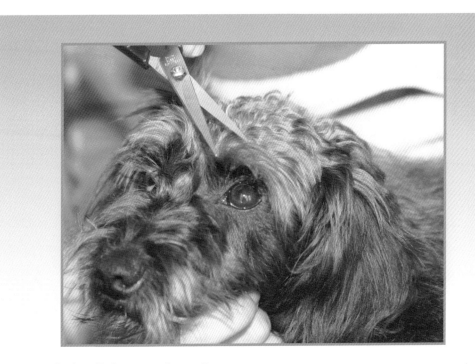

"Just a little off the top, please."

Schnoodle Safety

Safety precautions necessary for dog owners are very similar to those taken by parents of infants and young children. Begin with doggie-proofing the room in which your puppy will be allowed to run and play. Do this *before* you even bring the puppy home from the breeder. If your kitchen is to become the puppy room, make certain that the puppy can't get into any house-cleaning materials in open-floor shelves, cabinets, etc. The same applies outside your home in the area of your yard where you intend to take the puppy for house-training. Make sure no plants (indoors and outdoors) are within easy puppy reach, as some plants are toxic and you can be sure that the pup will want to taste them if he can. A listing of toxic plants and other unsafe substances for dogs is available on the Animal Poison Control Center page of the ASPCA's website (*www.aspca.org*). Also, remove fallen branches from the area and make sure that there are no puddles or other unsafe sources of water where the pup might find a drink. Puppies are curious creatures, so when it comes to safety, it is always better to be safe than to be sorry!

Beware a snooping Schnoodle!
Keep both eyes on your dog—indoors and out.

Tidy dogs agree...

House-training the
Schnoodle

Methods used by dog owners to housebreak their pets have run the gamut over the past decades, ranging from covering the floor of one room in the house with newspapers (and hoping for the best) to confining the pet in a cramped cage for hours on end and calling it "crate-training." All too often, the terms "house-training," "crate-training" and "housebreaking" have been mistakenly thought to be synonymous. Effective house-training of puppies is actually a two-stage process: first, employing a modern method of crate-training, followed by housebreaking.

Modern crate-training is based in part on a dog's natural instinct to avoid soiling his "den," if at all possible. The den in this situation, of course, is the crate. Simplistically speaking, that is the basis of crate-training. However, what many inexperienced dog owners forget is that if a puppy or unknowing adult dog really has to go potty, he *will* go wherever he is, including inside the crate. In application, crate-training a puppy involves taking him outside, either to an enclosed, safe yard (or over to his potty pad if indoor training is required, as in the case of city-dwellers) or to the curbside on leash, on a frequent, regular basis during the owner's waking hours and encouraging the pup to "go potty" in his designated place. Once the puppy has relieved himself outside in his area or on the pad indoors, he can have a supervised play/interaction period if the owner has the

crates are great!

"Some privacy, please?"

time to spare or the puppy can be put (back) inside the crate with a few toys to entertain himself. As long as the puppy is taken to where he's supposed to go potty on an adequate, regular schedule, he is not likely to soil his crate. After many weeks have passed and the puppy continually has not soiled his crate, even as the owner has progressively decreased the frequency with which the puppy has been taken outside to go potty and increased the amount of out-of-crate time, the owner (and puppy) are ready to graduate to the next step in the house-training process—housebreaking.

Housebreaking is an extension of crate-training. Once the puppy has consistently shown that he is able to refrain from going potty in his crate, then it's time to give the pup a larger living area in which to remain clean. This larger area could be a tile- or linoleum-floored kitchen that has been puppy-proofed and partitioned off with an adjustable-width baby gate or any similar room in which the puppy can still receive fairly frequent interaction with people during waking hours. The owner can even start out with setting up an exercise pen (typically a 3-foot-high model is adequate) in a room deemed safe for the puppy, just in case he "relapses" and goes potty on the floor! The puppy's crate should still be made available to him in this new space, but the crate door should be left open until the puppy's bedtime at night.

The owner still has to take the puppy outside to go potty on a regular schedule, from the first thing in the morning until the last thing that's done before the owner goes to bed at night. By now, however, the amount of time between the potty trips during the day has increased to four or maybe five hours. Gradually, over time, as the pup shows his ability to stay clean in that space, the owner can then graduate him to an even larger amount of living space. Perhaps the baby gate can be moved to a different doorway to add an adjacent (and of course puppy-proofed) room of the house to the puppy's living quarters. And

so it goes, over a few more months. About the earliest a dog owner can honestly expect to have a fully house-trained pet is when the pup is at least six months of age.

Just like children, every puppy is different. Some puppies catch on earlier than others and some a little later. The most important points in house-training a Schnoodle are to remain consistent with the training schedule throughout and to remain patient and fair with the puppy. Your Schnoodle puppy is probably a good bit smarter than you'd care to imagine!

Fenced yard, doggie door and an owner who is amazed by her well-trained Schnoodle.

A trained Schnoodle is an enjoyable companion...

Obedience Training the
Schnoodle

Having a Schnoodle puppy
and raising him through adulthood can be a
wonderful experience. However, if the puppy is
given no schooling, he will quickly grow up to
become a less-than-desirable member of the family. Because dogs
have formidable teeth and hard nails, the property damage that
an untrained or out-of-control dog (of almost any age or breed)
is capable of doing can be catastrophic.

Here's one of thousands of tales of doggie teeth. An owner
(who shall go unnamed!) came home one day and, upon opening
the front door, saw a trail of splintered wood across her family
room. She had left a 3-pound Toy Poodle locked in a downstairs
bathroom. The Poodle had clawed and chewed her way *through*
a wooden door, leaving a gaping hole! The entire door and door
frame had to be replaced. There is another account of an owner
who left her Rottweiler puppy tied to a coffee table while she left
the room. The rope that anchored the puppy to the coffee table
left him within chewing distance of a very expensive rattan
rocking chair. By the time the owner came back into the room,
the rocking chair was minus one rocker. One of the worst reports
I have heard came from an acquaintance of mine who left her
dog in her car while she ran into a store. When she came back
out to her car after just a short time, the dashboard of the car

with a smiling, happy owner.

had been literally chewed off, as had the inner lining of the passenger-side door. This is just another reason (of many) not to leave a dog unattended in a car; it can be dangerous...and expensive.

On a different note, there are the very sad stories of

The bells chime at potty time...

puppies who run outside through open front doors and are hit by cars in their own driveways or in the street just a short distance from home. Even dogs who are seemingly trained to stay with their owners, meaning those who usually come to their owners when called, have been killed instantly after chasing a squirrel or a cat into the street. Not listening to and not obeying a command *just that one time* can make the difference between having a dog for a long time and losing him forever.

If owning and training a dog was as easy to do as keeping a house plant, many more people would have dogs, and most dogs would be well trained and obedient. However, training a dog is an ongoing endeavor and needs to be started when the puppy is first adopted from the breeder. The longer the interim between bringing your puppy home and starting his training, the greater the opportunity the puppy will have to learn *bad* behaviors and get into mischief. When first training a puppy or dog, it is much harder if you have to first undo bad behavior before being able to begin teaching good behavior. A new puppy is virtually a clean slate upon which a new owner can impress proper behavior. Teaching your puppy the basic, yet most valuable, lessons first is crucial in serving as a foundation for the pup to learn more intricate commands later on.

The four most funda-mental commands (those which *all* dogs should know and follow implicitly) are "come," "sit," "down" and "stay." Since Schnoodles are half Miniature Schnauzer and half Poodle—both breeds that are known for their superior intelligence and ability to learn—training a Schnoodle in these basic commands should be a relatively simple process. Schnoodles are smart, eager pupils, willing and able to process and learn a variety of simple commands and, later, more complicated tricks. Once these four commands have

been learned, are understood and are heeded immediately and reliably, your puppy or dog will have the building blocks for becoming an obedient and well-behaved member of your family and of society in general. Following are some ways to teach these commands to your dog. When training a puppy, limit the training time; puppies have very short attention spans, and learning should be kept fun for everyone involved.

Training molds a dog into a mannerly family member and an all-around good canine citizen.

COME

The come command is the most important command of all. This command can save a dog's life during an emergency situation. Although come is one of the more difficult commands to teach a dog, it's best to teach it first and foremost while a puppy is still quite young and is at the stage in life when he wants to be with his human at all times. Always use your puppy's or dog's name in conjunction with the come command; for example, "Come, Biscuit." Never say the word "come" unless you are absolutely sure that your puppy is paying attention to you. Otherwise, the command word will become virtually meaningless to your dog, or worse yet, your dog will think he has an option!

Thus the best way to teach the come command to your puppy is to first put a collar on him (after you have already familiarized the puppy with wearing a collar), then attach a very long (10 to 15 feet), thin leash or cord to it. While holding the other end of the leash/cord, allow the puppy to move away from you. Then say, "Come, Biscuit." If your puppy comes to

Reward your Schnoodle
with a fun game of tug.

you on his own, give lots of happy praise. Occasionally you can give a small food reward. If the puppy chooses not to come to you at the first command, slowly start to pull the puppy toward you, continuing to say, "Come, Biscuit." When the puppy is by your side, praise him as though he made the choice to come to you on his own. Always reward your puppy with praise when he comes to you after you give the command with his name, even if he had no choice in the matter at all.

If your puppy is not tethered by a leash or long line and he has the choice to either disobey or ignore you, do *not* use the come command. Instead, you can either call him just by saying his name or you can clap your hands. You can even use a squeaky toy to get his attention, but do not say "Come" unless you are absolutely certain that your puppy has no choice but to come to you. If this method of training is used consistently, you will have a dog who will come to you every single time you use the command. This could save your dog's life if he happens to be off leash in a dangerous situation.

Reward your obedient buddy with a game of fetch.

SIT

The sit command is the second most important command to teach your puppy. It can be taught in conjunction with the come command. Puppies and dogs can learn more than one thing at a time. Like children, they are learning all the time, both good things and bad things. However, you want them to be learning many more of the *good* things! This will leave them little or no time to deviate and get into mischief.

The sit command is essentially the easiest of all to teach a puppy. Stand over the puppy while having him look up at you and say "Sit" as you push down on the puppy's hindquarters to coax him to sit down. Just like when you were teaching your puppy the come command, praise the puppy as if he did it all by himself. Although praise is always used as a reward, tiny bits of food treats can occasionally be given along with verbal praise.

For the first few training sessions, offer praise and reward even if the puppy does not obey the command all on his own. Stop the training session after a few minutes. Come back to the training later on in the day or wait until the following day to resume. Always remember to keep the training sessions short and fun. Practicing a particular command five to six times is usually sufficient at each session. You will be amazed at how fast your puppy will remember a command and be willing and eager to perform.

Elsie is so excited about her lessons
that she just can't sit down!

Down

Once the sit command has been mastered, move on to the down command. Have the puppy assume the sitting position. Then, at the same time that you are voicing the down command, gently pull the puppy's front legs forward so that he is forced to lie down. Give him extravagant praise as soon as he is lying down. Allow the puppy to get up and then command the puppy to come to you. After praising him when he reaches you, command the puppy to sit and then repeat the down command, once again stretching out the puppy's front legs in front of him to require him to lie down on his belly. Do this five or six times, following each repetition with lots of praise. When the session of repetitions is complete, reward your puppy with play time, with no training involved whatsoever; it can't be all work and no play!

Enjoying some "down" time.

STAY

The stay command is the last of the four basic obedience commands that you should teach your puppy. This is because the stay command is, shall we say, "attached at the hip" with the sit and the down commands. Once you know that your puppy has fully learned the sit and down commands and will do each one whenever the command is given, you can begin incorporating the stay command. For example, tell your puppy to sit. After the puppy sits properly, you immediately give the stay command. Of course, the puppy will not know initially what you mean by this new command, and he will attempt to get up. Calmly repeat the "sit and stay" commands at this time. If the puppy sits and stays seated for a few seconds, give lots of praise and maybe a reward. Continue to tell the puppy to sit, adding the stay command until the puppy is sitting and staying for at least a few seconds each time. Again, follow up the correct behavior with praise and possibly a reward.

The amount of time that the puppy remains seated after the sit/stay command is given should be increased as the training sessions continue. If this lesson is conducted consistently for both the

"Not only am I beautiful, but look how well I stay!"

Sitting, staying and looking so precious.

sit and down commands, a puppy or dog can be taught to sit and stay or lie down and stay for long periods of time. The stay command, like the come command, is vital to the safety of your puppy or dog. Imagine the scenario in which your dog is off leash and has inadvertently crossed a street but wants to get back to you. He might try darting through heavy traffic to reach you, but he knows the stay command, so you can order him to sit and stay, and he would stay in position until you could get to him. The down/stay and sit/stay commands are both vital to your dog's safety and well-being, as well as for *your* own peace of mind.

Controlling Bad Behavior with Commands

After your Schnoodle (and you) have learned the four basic commands, it will become so much easier for you to control any bad behaviors that your puppy or dog may exhibit, such as jumping on people, jumping on furniture, running out the front door, etc. A dog cannot be doing two behaviors simultaneously! If a dog jumps up on a guest who just came into your home, using the sit command will immediately have your dog sitting instead of jumping. If a visitor is fearful of dogs, giving your dog the down/stay command will make the dog seem far less threatening.

A busy Schnoodle is a Schnoodle that stays out of trouble.

You walk your Schnoodle, not the
other way around.

LEASH TRAINING

Too many dogs aren't taught to properly walk on a leash. In so many cases seen on the street every day, it appears as though the dog is walking the person instead of the other way around. It is a simple matter to teach a dog to correctly walk on leash. From day one of taking your puppy out onto the public sidewalk, after he has received the last of his puppy immunizations, put the collar on your puppy, attach a 6-foot leash and make sure that the puppy walks on your left side, immediately next to your left leg. If the puppy tries to run or walk ahead of you, stop walking and bring the puppy back to your left side. Do not continue walking unless the puppy is walking next to you. The puppy will soon understand that if he wants to move ahead or get anywhere at all, he must stay directly by your side. This is the beginning of leash training. It is far easier to start off doing it correctly than to allow your puppy to run all over and then have to retrain him.

It's a special bond when your dog looks up to you as his leader.

BEYOND THE BASICS

Once your Schnoodle knows the basics you can consider going on to more advanced training. There are obedience classes in which trainers teach the *owners* to train their own dogs. Many books have been published on this subject, with many different methods being expounded. There are probably as many ways to train a dog as there are trainers who practice the methods and write the books! Some methods use only verbal praise. Some methods use only treat rewards. Some methods use both praise and treat rewards. There are trainers who use the clicker method, which is another way of getting a dog to understand that a reward will be forthcoming. I liken clicker training to Pavlov's method of getting a dog to salivate. Every time he was about to give his dogs a treat, Pavlov rang a bell. After a while, the bell sound caused the dogs to salivate. This is essentially the basis of clicker training. When your dog does something correctly, the clicker sound is made, and the dog then receives a reward or treat. After a while, the dog associates the clicker sound with a forthcoming reward, and he thus knows that the sound of the clicker indicates he has done something correctly.

A well-trained Schnoodle is like a good child. He will be there, happy to do what you ask of him, waiting for a cue, a look or a verbal message. Such a dog is a pleasure to be around, and all who meet him will remark that they wish they had a dog just like him. He is the dog or puppy who walks next to his owner, not the one dragging his owner down the street. This is the Schnoodle whose owner can leave him home alone for a time, knowing that the dog will do no damage to the house he lives in. He can be faithfully trusted with children and adults alike. He will sit and stay in response to either a verbal command or a hand signal. The well-trained Schnoodle will not get up or walk away until given permission to do so.

There are actually many such dogs of different breeds. We see them all the time, serving as guide dogs for the blind, as therapy dogs, as agility dogs and as herding dogs. While certain breeds of dog may have a reputation for higher intelligence than other breeds, most dogs are capable of being trained to do anything asked of them, given enough time, patience and an owner with a bit of knowledge of how to approach the basic training. There are so many things that dogs are capable of learning, remembering and doing. It is truly sad when a dog is purchased or adopted as a pet but then simply left to his own devices by an inattentive owner. The best dogs, the type who become beloved members of the family and seem to be near-human, are those who are given the time, patience, training and love to which all creatures of this kind are entitled. Hopefully, if you are reading this book, you are one of these owners who cares enough about his Schnoodle to train him to become an obedient dog and a great canine member of society.

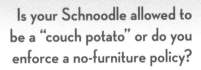

Is your Schnoodle allowed to be a "couch potato" or do you enforce a no-furniture policy?

Family fun is even more fun...

The number of games that

you can play and activities that you can do with your Schnoodle is essentially limited only by your own imagination and the willingness of your Schnoodle to join in. In most canine activities, dog and owner participate together, so the two of you must have a good bond and must work well together. Like most other things in life, the basics of obedience must first be learned to serve as the strong foundation on which all other aspects of a good dog/owner relationship can be built. This includes sound knowledge and reliable execution of the four basic commands (come, sit, down and stay), as well as walking properly on leash and following commands both on and off leash. What better way to teach and build your bond at the same time than by employing some simple games or fun activities as a form of reward during training?

Say, for example, that you have only recently brought your puppy home from the breeder. Even though you are basically restricted by the crate-training schedule to having playtime indoors (after the puppy has gone potty outdoors), you can start teaching your puppy the sit and stay commands simultaneously. The process of learning these two commands can be made more pleasurable for both you and the puppy with a game called "treasure hunt."

when shared with a Schnoodle!

Get your puppy into the sit position and place a favorite toy or small treat within his sight. Keep the puppy sitting and staying for a moment, then release him to go get the toy or treat (either by physically letting go of him or by saying "Okay" if the puppy will stay in the sit position on his own). Repeat this exercise just a few times during each play/training period by placing the toy or treat in different locations at increasing distances from the puppy. Once the puppy gets the hang of this game, you can start placing more than one treasure for the pup to find. Other basic commands can be taught simultaneously in a similar fun teaching manner.

As your puppy gets older, and the both of you are more confident of his learning ability and pleased with his achievements thus far, you can start attending puppy classes toward the goal of earning the American Kennel Club's (AKC) Canine Good Citizen® (CGC)

Schnoodle sitting pretty...

and Schnoodle flying high!

award and other obedience achievements. Even though the AKC does not count the Schnoodle among its recognized breeds, it encourages pure-bred and mixed-breed dogs alike to attend and complete the CGC program. Regardless of what you hope to achieve, puppy classes are excellent for reinforcing commands already taught as well as learning new ones, all while socializing with the other dogs, owners and trainers. The socialization is as much, if not more, a benefit as the training! This is an ideal program to begin after your young dog has received all of his puppy immunizations and his first rabies shot.

Once your dog has earned his CGC certification, you might consider expanding his (and your own) social-interaction skills through therapy-dog training and work. Therapy dogs and handlers are highly trained teams who visit nursing homes, hospitals and other institutions to offer companionship and comfort to patients and long-term residents. This volunteer program, which emphasizes the friendly, mild-mannered temperament of the therapy dogs, has been proven to promote healing and emotional well-being, elevating the quality of life for both the residents visited and the staff members who care for these people (not to mention how much your Schnoodle will enjoy the attention and how good it will make you feel to volunteer!). A premiere therapy-dog program/organization is Therapy Dog International, Inc. (TDI), which can be found online at www.tdi-dog.org. For a dog to be considered for TDI, he must be at least one year old and have his CGC certification; he then must pass an evaluation that tests his temperament as well as his reactions to sights, sounds and goings-on commonly encountered in a healthcare environment. As with the CGC program, TDI welcomes both pure-bred and mixed-breed dogs as therapy-dog candidates.

Another activity closely involving both the dog and owner is agility competition. Dog agility competition, which began in England in 1978, is an exciting show of speed, strength, coordination and…well…agility, pitting the dog and the handler against the clock to achieve the fastest time in completing a difficult obstacle course. The dog must follow cues given by his handler as the handler runs beside him through the course to the finish line. Training for agility competition (and naturally, running the course) can be hard work initially but greatly strengthens the relationship between dog and handler and offers both a great deal of fun and exercise for both. Various organizations across North America, such as the United States Dog Agility Association, Inc., the American Mixed Breed Obedience Registration, the United Kennel Club and the North American Dog Agility Council, Inc., sponsor canine agility competitions open to all kinds of dogs, each with different types of obstacle courses and various classes based largely on different skill levels and dog sizes (*not* by breed). Depending on the type of course, obstacles can include combinations of weave poles, see-saws, tunnels, jumps, etc. Because the Schnoodle is not AKC-recognized, he cannot compete in AKC trials or earn AKC agility titles. The other organizations, however, do offer competition and titles for all dogs.

It's Scout, in the role of "Schnoodle Claus."

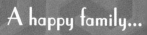
A happy family...

Health Concerns for Schnoodle Owners

You certainly know about hybrid vigor, although not in great detail. It has long been said by many people, including some breeders and veterinarians, that mutts make the best pets. They are long-lived, usually healthy and do not seem to have as many inherited or genetic maladies as are seen in many of the pure-bred lines. Some dictionaries define hybrid vigor, or outbreeding enhancement, as "heterosis, an increased strength of different characteristics in hybrids; the possibility to obtain a 'better' individual by combining the virtues of its parents."

Not all such crossings produce better offspring. Sometimes certain crossings produce inferior offspring, with hybrids inheriting traits that would make them unfit for survival. It is only when the hybrid is superior to its parents that the term "hybrid vigor" is used. While Poodles and Miniature Schnauzers are both wonderful pure-breds, each has its own set of genetic problems and some behavior issues. The cross of a Miniature Schnauzer and Poodle, however, seems to produce a hybrid with the better attributes of both parent breeds (i.e., hybrid vigor).

Although Schnoodles have not been bred to the same extent or for as long as some other crossbreeds, all indications so far are positive with respect to health, temperament, looks and other factors. Of course, using only the best, healthiest examples of

with a healthy Schnoodle.

Lilly is full of Schnoodle vigor.

both parent breeds will help to ensure that the resulting Schnoodles remain as they are now: healthy, well adjusted and free from genetic disorders.

Given that you have done your homework properly as the new owner of a Schnoodle puppy, meaning that you have found an excellent breeder and chosen a puppy that is healthy, examined by your vet, and seemingly free from any troubling maladies, it is time to bring the new puppy home and start him on a program to ensure his future health and well-being. The breeder should have supplied you with a health record when you took your puppy home; this will document all veterinary visits, medications and vaccinations your puppy has received since birth. This record should document the types of vaccinations and wormings, and dates administered, along with information on any medications given (including the labels from the bottles, if available). The health record should also have information as to when the next vaccinations are due, as well as any other information or tips that might be helpful to the new owner.

Most eight-week-old puppies have received at least one, or perhaps two, of the series of puppy immunizations necessary to protect against the most dangerous illnesses, including parvovirus, parainfluenza, distemper and canine hepatitis. These shots are the start of a series of vaccinations. It is necessary for the puppy to receive the entire series in order to have full protection. Although some veterinarians follow a slightly different immunization schedule, these shots are typically given at 6, 8, 10, 12 and 16 weeks of age. If puppies are raised in cities, they should not be taken to public parks or walked on city streets until the entire complement of shots has been given. Puppies under 16 weeks of age are highly susceptible to parvovirus, distemper and various other diseases.

Puppies should be wormed at two, four, six and eight weeks of age for roundworms, parasitic nematodes commonly found in most dogs. If the breeder has the adult dogs on a worming program and all are free of worms, it will still behoove the breeder to prophylactically worm the puppies. Whereas adult dogs may test worm-free, if the mother dog ever had roundworms, even as a puppy, juvenile stages of these worms will lay dormant in the mother dog's body tissues. When the mother dog becomes pregnant and certain hormones are emitted into her system, the worms become energized and migrate into the bloodstream, thence traveling to the puppies by way of the umbilical cord. Many puppies are born with worms already in their systems.

There are other types of worms that can invade a puppy's intestinal system as well: hookworms, whipworms, tapeworms and pinworms. Some of these worm types are transmitted from the mother dog. Others are transmitted by

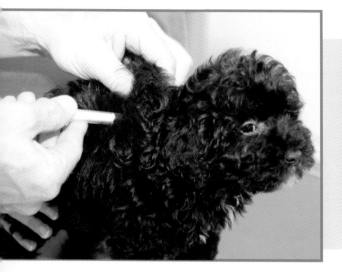

Vaccinations take over where the mother's milk leaves off in providing immunity.

mosquitoes (e.g., heart-worms), by sniffing or eating feces from dogs who are infected with worms or by finding and eating feces from other animals such as rabbits, deer, etc.

It would be wise to ask the breeder if your puppy has been examined by the breeder's own vet. Many states in the US, such as New York, require this by law. All puppies must have a veterinary health certificate and be at least eight weeks of age before being shipped by air. Some vets give a cursory examination, but it is a good idea for the buyer to ask the breeder to have the puppy checked by a vet prior to shipping or prior to your picking him up as an added measure of buyer protection. The examining veterinarian should write and sign a letter describing what he has checked for and what was found.

Most puppies are weaned from their mothers at six weeks of age and can safely go to their new homes by eight weeks of age. There are exceptions to this rule. Very

Listening for a healthy heart.

tiny puppies (under 3 pounds) can be overly stressed by a long plane ride or car trip. Some of these puppies can become hypoglycemic, a condition in which the levels of blood sugar become critically low. Puppies with this condition can succumb and die very quickly. A conscientious breeder is aware of this danger and will keep very small puppies until they reach a higher weight or until they are older, usually 10 to 12 weeks of age, before allowing them to leave.

We have talked about checking out the breeder, what to look for and what questions to ask. There are valid reasons for doing this. Dogs can contract a myriad of parasites (e.g., worms, protozoa, mites) and infections in the short time between birth and eight weeks of age, the time when most puppies are ready and able to go to their new homes. I will elaborate on some of the things that the buyer should be looking for. This list can be used as a quick reference guide to aid in choosing a good puppy.

Feeling the belly for signs of internal parasites.

WORMS

Suspect *roundworms* if the puppies are pot-bellied or have dull coats. Worms take the nutrition out of whatever food the puppy is eating. If a puppy is infested with worms, he will be eating but getting very little of the nutrients needed for growth. Once worms mature (and this happens within a matter of weeks), they fill the puppy's digestive tract in the belly, and the puppy will not feel like eating. Worms also migrate through the puppy's body, entering the lungs and causing coughing. This coughing is sometimes mistaken for kennel cough. Suspect *tapeworms* if you see fleas on the puppies. Fleas carry tapeworms. Tapeworms attach to the intestinal lining, feeding on the nutrients being digested by the puppy. Tapeworm segments can also be passed in the feces of adult dogs and older pups. These motile segments, which look like grains of rice, are actually egg sacs. Dog or puppies sniff the feces or ingest these sacs and become infested or reinfested with the tapeworms. Pay close attention to the area where the puppies are housed, and ask to see where they are allowed to go out and play. If these areas are not clean, suspect that the puppies are not getting proper care.

Cleanliness is of utmost importance when raising puppies and should weigh heavily when choosing a puppy or a breeder. The manner in which a puppy starts his life means a great deal. It can be the difference between bringing home a healthy puppy and getting a good start or bringing home a sickly puppy who may have permanent damage that will show up later on in life, not to mention hefty vet bills.

The whole litter goes to visit the vet before they go to new homes...and so should your new pup.

SKIN MITES

Check the puppy's coat and skin. If the hair feels greasy and there is substantial dandruff present, the puppy could be harboring skin mites. Watch the puppies at play or rest. Are any of them scratching? Puppies will scratch if they have skin mites, mange mites, lice or fleas. Although mange mites are too small to be seen without a microscope, signs like severe dandruff and a dull or greasy-feeling coat can be indicative of an infestation. There are two types of mange: sarcoptic and demodectic. Sarcoptic mange is passed from dog to dog, and the mites can survive off a host for a number of days. It is curable with shampoos, dips and medication. These mites can be passed to humans as well. Demodectic mange is passed on from the dam, and it is more difficult to cure. Suspect demodectic mange if the puppy is very young and exhibits symptoms of mange. This is another very good reason to want to see the dam. If she is healthy-looking with a shiny coat, clear eyes and a happy attitude, the chances of getting a good, healthy puppy are much better.

PROTOZOA

Plan on spending time when choosing or picking up your puppy. You will want to see your puppy defecate while you are there. Young puppies have numerous bowel movements per day, and the chances are high that your puppy, possibly all of the puppies in the litter, will have bowel movements during playtime. You will want to see that the puppy's stool has a firm shape with no signs of diarrhea or blood.

A healthy mouth is important to your Schnoodle's overall health...be a good doggie dentist.

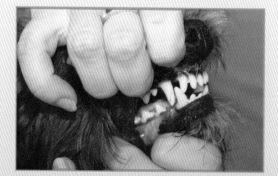

Never take home a puppy if you suspect or see that the puppy has diarrhea. No reputable breeder would allow a puppy to leave the premises if he has diarrhea, is vomiting or is coughing. Blood in the stool can signify either worm infestation or other conditions brought on by protozoa in the intestinal tract.

You know that chew toys help keep your Schnoodle's teeth healthy, and he thinks that they are just plain fun!

Protozoa are one-celled organisms that invade the intestinal tract, multiply rapidly and cause bloody or gelatinous stools. One of these protozoa is called *Coccidia*; the other is *Giardia*. Both are water-borne and can be picked up from ground water, well water, an infected mother dog or infected surroundings. These protozoa are insidious. They cannot be seen and sometimes puppies can harbor them and show no outward signs of carrying them. A strong, healthy puppy can, and will, develop resistance to these protozoa. Puppies weakened from lack of good food, from being infested with worms, from being stressed out due to shipping or from going to new homes and becoming overtired from not getting enough rest can succumb to these protozoa and become very ill or die. Many breeders routinely give medication for coccidian protozoa if they think there is a chance that their pups or adult dogs might harbor them. If a breeder gives you medicine to give to your puppy, suspect that the puppy has one of these conditions. Albon™ is the medicine of choice for *Coccidia*; Flagyl™ is the medicine given for *Giardia*. Both medicines are extremely effective.

COUGHING, COLDS AND VIRUSES

Puppies do not get colds like we do. If a puppy has mucus coming from his nose, if his eyes are runny or crusted or if these symptoms are combined with diarrhea and/or vomiting, suspect distemper, a highly contagious virus that can be life-threatening. If a puppy is lethargic, vomiting and has bloody diarrhea, suspect parvovirus, often called "parvo," a virulent virus that is life-threatening to most puppies. If a puppy is coughing, suspect kennel cough, which can be either viral or bacterial. If bacterial, kennel cough can be treated with antibiotics. If viral, the cough must run its course. With veterinary treatment and care, most pups or dogs with kennel cough recover easily and quickly, but kennel cough is contagious.

If you are visiting a kennel or home-based breeding establishment and you do not feel comfortable for any reason, do not purchase your puppy there. Remember, you may need help with your puppy in the future and you want to trust as well as have a good rapport with the person from whom you are buying.

SPAYING/NEUTERING

Another important consideration is spaying and neutering. Good breeders will ask their buyers if they want to purchase a puppy as a pet or if they are contemplating breeding their dog at some future time. Most buyers are simply looking for a family pet, and family pets should be spayed (if female) or neutered (if male). There are many vets and breeders who feel that without doing these procedures, dogs are more prone to diseases. Of course this is true and it makes sense. If a female dog has no uterus, she cannot succumb to uterine cancer or ovarian cancer. She will be much less likely to get cancer of the mammary glands as well. Male dogs that are neutered cannot get testicular cancer. There are other valid reasons for spaying or neutering, too. Although we all think that we can watch over our dogs constantly, this is not always the case. Intact male dogs tend to roam. Female dogs in season must be constantly watched over so they do not get together with a male dog. Females remain in season for up to three weeks. This can occur twice a year. As a pet owner, it is far easier to not have to deal with these things. A good breeder will try to steer new owners toward spaying or neutering their new puppy; some will even have a spay/neuter clause in their sales agreement.

In the case of a crossbreed such as a Schnoodle, more knowledge is necessary when contemplating breeding. Breeding a Miniature Schnauzer to a Poodle is first-generation breeding, and the offspring will be Schnoodles, 50% Poodle and 50% Miniature Schnauzer. Once you take two first-generation Schnoodles (even the finest, healthiest examples) and breed them to one another, you are playing with genes that are not "set." The resulting second-generation puppies could look like Schnoodles, Miniature Schnauzers or Poodles. Second-generation breeding is essentially a crapshoot. It can and should be done only by knowledgeable breeders who understand the variables and who have a definite reason to produce second-generation puppies (i.e., to continue the lines and establish a breed of dog that is no longer a crossbreed). This takes much knowledge and record-keeping and also requires an understanding of the ancestry of the dogs being used to start a new breed. Schnoodles are not a "breed" of dog. They are still a crossbreed. They will continue to be a crossbreed until one or more dedicated breeders breed unrelated healthy pairs of Schnoodles for eight or more generations, keeping meticulous records and ensuring that the resulting puppies are "pure-bred." We discuss breeding in more detail in the next chapter.

Breeding means effort, care, work, dedication...

Breeding the
Schnoodle

G reat care must be taken in

selecting the very best representatives, or candidates, of the chosen breeds when contemplating breeding a pair of dogs, be they members of the same breed to produce like pure-breds or pure-breds of different breeds to produce crossbreeds or hybrids. After all, "What goes in, comes out." Certain characteristics, be they physical or mental, are inherited—genetically programmed—carried from parents to offspring. A good Schnoodle breeder will, therefore, want to choose the healthiest, best-looking and most temperamentally sound dogs from both parent breeds when deciding to breed Schnoodles.

Unlike mutts, whose parentage cannot be traced back and examined, breeding pure-breds gives the breeder a chance to check into the lineages of the parent dogs. There is much that a breeder can find out, from physical characteristics like colors and sizes to genetic health issues, such as eye disorders, hip dysplasia, skin disorders, etc. Good breeders keep records of puppies they have raised and sold, and honest breeders will make these facts known. Any breeder who sells puppies should make the distinction between puppies that are being sold as pets and need to be neutered or spayed and puppies that are being sold as future or potential breeding stock. In the latter case, only puppies who are the best examples of their breed and who come from long lines of dogs that are problem-free should be sold to those who intend to breed. To do *less* would be unethical.

and sweet moments.

All first-generation (F_1) Schnoodles are the result of outcrossing bloodlines. No buyer need ask or wonder if first-generation Schnoodle puppies are inbred; since two distinct breeds of dog are being mated to each other, this precludes any chance of inbreeding or line-breeding as the dogs cannot be related to each other. This is a very good thing because many problems that plague pure-bred dogs are the direct result of inbreeding, either through ignorance or by design. Many of the serious problems found in pure-bred lines are the direct responsibility of unknowing or uncaring breeders. While many breeders of pure-bred dogs will expound on the "horror" of crossing pure-breds to synthesize these newer hybrid crosses, the fact is that all of today's recognized breeds started out as crossbreeds. That is the origin of all breeds of dog. Some even came from crosses using more than two breeds of dog.

The first, or start-up, generations of new breeds are usually the healthiest with the least inherited faults. This is due to the aforementioned hybrid vigor. Hybrid vigor does not mean that the dogs are more active. Vigor, in this sense, means that the gene pool has been renewed and that problems inherent in the parent breeds have much less chance of being passed on to the gene pool of the offspring because the genes responsible for certain conditions are not exactly the same in each breed. Hence, the genes do not combine to pass along the condition or problem in the new generation of offspring. Following this line of thought, if the very best parent dogs are used, the resulting Schnoodle offspring should be excellent-quality puppies and dogs. As in all breeding, the product of the equation is a reflection of the care given to the mother dog during pregnancy, the care given to the mother dog and puppies after birthing and the care given to the puppies once they are weaned from the mother and after being sold.

In the case of breeding a Poodle to a Miniature Schnauzer, some characteristics of the future puppies can be pre-

A lovely Giant Schnauzer dam with her prized brood.

planned. Certain color, size and disposition factors can be manipulated by the breeder. Since Poodles come in three sizes, the size of the Schnoodle puppies can be planned. By breeding a very tiny male Toy Poodle to a very small female Miniature Schnauzer, the likelihood of producing very small, toy-size Schnoodles would be highly favorable. The same would be true if larger Schnoodles were desired. A Miniature Schnauzer male could be bred to a Miniature or Standard Poodle female, and the resulting puppies would most likely grow to be larger in size. These scenarios, however, do not mean that all puppies in a litter would be small or large. There are always ancestral variables in the equation because many Toy and Miniature Poodles have been crossed over the years, and so there is always the chance that there will be quite a bit of variation among the sizes of pups, even those from the same litter. That is why a good breeder will never *guarantee* the adult size of a Poodle-cross puppy.

Once the parent dogs to be used for the mating have been selected, it is simply a matter of time and patience, waiting until the female comes into season. Most dogs come into heat every six months. This can vary, but twice a year is the general timetable for dogs. This is probably because conception from a heat in late winter would assure that pups would be born in the springtime when they would have the best chance of survival. Four months after the birth of a spring litter, the bitch would come back into estrus and could potentially breed for a second litter which would be due in late summer or early fall. These pups would also have ample time to mature before the weather would become too harsh. This is one of nature's ways of ensuring survival of a species. Because most breeding dogs live indoors and have been bred and raised as household pets, many dogs' heat cycles do not follow that rule. Some bitches come into heat very early on in life (at age six months or

so), while some come into heat well past a year of age. Some bitches come into heat every eight to ten months and some only come into heat once a year. A breeder should keep records of each breeding dog to know when her heat cycles are likely to happen. By doing this, vaccinations, wormings and other necessary procedures can be done in a safe and timely manner.

A breeder with more than one breeding bitch can choose the optimum time for each female dog to be bred so that there are not too many litters of puppies being born at one time. Puppies require time and attention. Too many litters born at one time or too closely together can make it very hard at weaning time when all of the pups need a great deal of attention and socialization

A good breeder tends to all of the pups' needs.

during the weeks prior to being placed in their new homes.

There is an optimum time when a female will allow a male to mate with her. This is usually between the 7th and 14th day of the estrous cycle. Again, this can vary from female to female, but if a female is not *ready* to be bred, she will not stand for the male dog. When the female is ready, she will let the male know by the process known as "flagging," whereby the female will put her tail to one side and allow the male access to her for the mating process.

At the optimum time for fertilization and conception, there is also a change in the flow and color of the female's discharge. The color of the discharge changes from a bright red to a lighter brown hue, and the flow lessens. The color and consistency of the discharge combined with the female's behaving in a receptive manner are what tell the breeder that the female is ready to be bred. This is the most effective time for conception. A female can remain receptive and fertile for a period of a day or more to a week or more. There are tests that can determine the most fertile period for breeding, but most breeders go by the two aforementioned guidelines, and most bitches become pregnant if they are healthy and there are no significant underlying problems.

Once a bitch has been bred and has gone out of heat, it is approximately two months until the puppies are due to be born, or whelped. Since there is no way of knowing exactly from which breeding or on which day the female became pregnant, it once again becomes a matter of good guessing. Bitches typically carry for 57 to 63 days. Most breeders count 57 days from the first mating and use that date as the due date. Some females can carry for up to 76 days from a one-time breeding date. This would be exceptional, but it has been known to happen. Miniature Schnauzers seem to carry for a longer term than some other breeds, and this has been our experience with our Miniature Schnauzers. However, this is not to say that all Miniature Schnauzers will do this.

BIRTH OF THE PUPPIES

When pregnancy nears the end of term, there are usually certain behaviors that alert the breeder to the fact that whelping time is near. Typically, a pregnant dog will stop eating a day or two before giving birth. She will start digging, trying to prepare a nest or bed for her soon-to-be-born puppies. Within 24 hours of delivery, the pregnant dog's body temperature will drop to below 100 degrees Fahrenheit. Within a very short time prior to delivery, the mother dog will begin to pant and will become very restless. These are all typical signs of the impending delivery of pups; however, sometimes a dog will exhibit few or none of these signs and still begin to deliver puppies.

Puppies develop in the two horns of the dog's uterus and are born sequentially from alternating sides. Puppies should be born head first, but many puppies are born breech (back legs first) and typically are born with little to no difficulty. Puppies are usually born enclosed in a placental sac, and each puppy has its own placenta or afterbirth. Some puppies come out without their sacs and these puppies do fine. If a puppy comes out in an intact sac and the sac is not removed immediately, the puppy will try to breathe and will unwittingly breathe in the placental fluid, thereby drowning in its own birth fluid. This is one reason why the breeder should always try to be there when a bitch is in labor. Many times puppies can be saved who would otherwise not survive. New mothers who have never delivered puppies may not have the innate instincts to immediately get the puppies out of their sacs, clean them and detach them from their placentas. It would be up to the breeder to intercede at this time and save any puppies that are not being cared for by the mother dog.

While to some, watching a dog give birth is thought of and talked about as something very wonderful and exciting to experience, in reality it can be very frightening, and knowledge and split-second decisions can mean the difference between puppies' living and dying. This is also true in the first days following the birth of the puppies. Too many times, mother dogs are overwhelmed by the sheer number of puppies and may inadvertently lie down on and crush one or more.

Occasionally weaker puppies are pushed away or move away from the mother dog. They can become chilled very quickly and easily. A chilled puppy cannot digest food even if it can muster enough strength to nurse.

Don't forget the Poodle dad!

A HEALTHY BROOD

Most litters of pups are multiple-birth litters. Nature intends this because puppies are so fragile when born, and the issue of "survival of the fittest" comes into play with any newborns. The strongest, healthiest puppies will always have the best chance for survival, and these will be the future parents of new generations. That is how a particular species thrives. This is very evident when watching puppies being born and growing up.

Puppies work very hard for the first few days and weeks of their lives to get the food they need to grow and flourish. Puppies are sightless when born, and their ears are closed. Closed eyes and ears are protection for the puppies as they rummage around in search of food and warmth. If dirt or bugs were to get into the eyes or ears of newborns, great damage could be done. Newborn puppies, kittens and other small mammals cannot protect themselves from injury, so Mother Nature makes sure that the eyes and ears of the puppies are closed off for approximately 14 days after whelping takes place. By the time the eyes and ears open, the puppies are essentially past the hardest part of their new lives, the time when they are the weakest and most vulnerable. The pups that make it past two weeks of age usually have a very good chance for survival.

Puppies do little more than nurse, sleep, nurse, sleep—with occasional potty time—for the first few weeks of their lives. The mother dog frequently cleans the puppies by licking them, and she keeps the den or whelping box clean using the same method. The licking of the puppies keeps their excretory organs functioning properly while helping to stimulate the puppies to pass urine and feces. She will continue to clean her puppies for the first few weeks of their lives. The puppies will start to interact with each other at about three weeks of age. That is the time when they begin to walk, toddling around and falling down just like human babies. By four weeks of age, the puppies are starting to sample their mother's food, play with toys, walk and pounce, growl and play-bite. It is at this stage that personalities begin to emerge.

When the puppies are between five to eight weeks of age, the breeder can begin to judge which puppies are the most outgoing, which puppies are the most mellow, etc. With this information, the breeder is better able to place puppies in the most suitable situations when they are old enough to go to new homes. While there are differences of opinion among breeders, trainers and behaviorists as to the correct age for separating puppies from their littermates, our experience watching over many litters of puppies tell us that when puppies reach approximately six weeks of age, the mother dog is leaving the puppies for longer and longer periods of time and is more and more unwilling to allow her puppies to nurse on her. Puppy teeth are very sharp, as are puppy toenails. With a few exceptions, pups are usually ready to leave for new homes at eight weeks old.

If the puppies are eating solid food well by six weeks of age, the weaning process begins. From then on, the puppies are fed twice daily and are kept meticulously clean. They are given various types of toys to play with, and they are introduced to many different sights and sounds. If the weather is mild, the puppies should go outside each day for a few hours so they can romp and play. Running and playing helps them develop their sense of balance, and it tires them out so they sleep well. It also aids their digestive processes. They instinctively begin to urinate and defecate outside, away from the areas where they eat and sleep. This is instinctual with young animals, and this instinct should be utilized as part of the training process.

Health Matters!

For potential owners, a good breeder's care and attention from before the mating takes place to after the puppies are placed in new homes give them an advantage in obtaining sound Schnoodle pups with the potential for long and healthy lives.

INDEX